Echoes From A Distant Drum

By

Thalamus' Ink.

1st Books - rev. 06/17/02

Acknowledgements

...

I watched her eyes dance across the pages. Her face was reflective of a myriad of emotions, and for that moment, I felt that our minds and souls had merged. The pinnacle of my exuberance was then...

I would like to thank friends who demonstrated "the patience of Job", when these works "voiced" needed an ear...

Ethel Parker, Charles and Beverly Alston, Patricia Canterbury, Gary and Sherry Perkins, Fred and Sandra Rose, Orie and Ola Brown, Larry Nazry, Marsha Nazry, Evelyn Dixon, Kermit Boston, Nathan Allen, Phillip Burgette, and Fahizah Alim.

A very special thanks to Ms. Mignon Hayes.

Also
Eyes on the Prize – With apologies to Mr. Juan Williams
Alone In Desolate Surroundings – Dedicated to Kedrick Brown

And by no means last nor least
Through Life's Cracked Door – to my Father – Edward Matthew Douglas
...

Telepathic imprints
Portend of deeds yet undone
Whispering hints of cerebral matter
Like echoes from a distant drum

Dedicated to my wife, Jessica

Who enriches my life.

Forward

Respect this place
Where I am free to expose
The joys and the burdens
Of this life's soul

Time
Quickly changes everything
Like soaps
Like coffees
Like guns
Like needs
Like speed
Like computers
Like commuters
Like the news
Like our views

During my lifetime
These ideas were formed
And I have written them to keep them indelible
They are the only things that I have to give
They are the only love that I have to give you

Do not confuse this
With the keys to a man's soul
For often performances have gone
Without Oscars
In times when
The flesh is disrobed
And the mind's intention
Is to fashion a weapon
And cast "love" to the weak

Why
Do you close your eyes
When you kiss?

Why
Do you trust love's blossom
To the darkness?
What you search for isn't me
But the soul of my brothers

Thalamus' Ink.

Table Of Contents

Yesterdays, Today and Tomorrows

Life's a rivers run
Full of life and full of fun
And a creek's dried bed

Thalamus' Ink.

Poetry

Saturated emotions
Penned with letters
Hung out on clotheslines
Scented by breezes
Dried by sunlight
And worn by nudes...

Thalamus' Ink.

Microns

Microns apart love and hate
One soothes
The other irritates

Microns apart hate and love
One pent up
The other as spacious as the sky above

Microns apart love and hate
One allows
The other disavows what we appreciate

Microns apart hate and love
Creating one thin line
From which the other is defined
And towards which we move

Thalamus' Ink.

Spring

When winter's coat is cast aside
And ridden out by a warming trend

When tropical rains make little buds strain
And birds and bees abide again

When we can consume nature's sweet perfumes
The scents arouse our senses

When every day presents the pleasure of you
And our minds are without fences

Spring is your vibrance
Spring is your temperate temporal changes

Spring is the warmth you are
And I wouldn't rearrange this

Spring is only one third of your beauty
It's all that they can see

The other two thirds don't require words
It's what you share with me

Thalamus' Ink.

Charmed

Deep red velvety blossom
Upon kelly's green prickly pedestal
Still regal in aspect and allure
Seductive fragrance, oh haunting aroma
Lifting bridges heavenward
Inspiring and inspiring

Mated at first touch
My inquisitive fumbling
And you're stinging barbs
Each designed
To keep the other near

Thalamus' Ink.

Blind

You looked for love
Though it encircled you like the wind
You had but to breathe
Or lift your head
To anticipate its appointment
But undiscerning – you fled

You looked for love
In a mink
In a diamond
Using the one sense
Neglecting the others
Five far more profound

You looked for love
In Mardi Gras and Time Square
In Rio
In Paris
Everywhere
Oblivious that it might be wise
Just to sit still
And close your eyes
To see

Thalamus' Ink.

Missing You

Constraints
Of time and distance
Confine
Our conversations and rendezvous

In your absence
Memory bridges this abyss
In my life

Presenting a path of hope
That our reunion
Is just within the next step
And I…
Am in midstride

Thalamus' Ink.

Captured

My eyes were betrayed
For you weren't there
My gaze was stayed
Through the rain filled air
Which couldn't wash you from my mind
For insight is eyesight
To the blind

Incessant excitement and anticipation
Loving
Losing
Then love's reaffirmation
Truly is a tethered relation
Whose distance from then till now
Has extended from days to months somehow

Your name's just the other side of these lips
Which unrewarded still crave your kiss
Your kindred soul which if set free
Would find its way right back to me
And mine to you my lady fair
But needing vessels to bring them there
Just like dandelions ferried by air

The terms of our imprisonment
Having accounted for these events
Leave us
Sad and longing…

Thalamus' Ink.

The Chameleon's Cage

A golden glow embraces you
In this shadow shrouded rendezvous
Secreting lovers for many ages
Muffling hushed tones and murmured phrases

Momentarily, time's concentrate
Is a palisade between us and fate
Warding off worlds and others
This fragile fortress designed for lovers

Altered fantasies and goals
Willing acceptance to what unfolds
Shipwrecked upon this "hallowed ground"
With high tides rising all around

And yet she comes to me
Knowing full well discoveries fee
And I to her, and no less bold
If only the moment to behold

The aura of her silhouette
Touched me long before we met
This gentle breeze that fills my sails
Sustaining us til evening pales

The kindly aspect of her eyes
Know of pain and paradise
And utter more than mouths express
Having both roads traveled more or less

My Cherie – our love is flawed
For outer worlds can't be ignored
Our perfect union of soma and souls
In morning assumes other roles

If we know why the caged bird sings
Open the door and give it wings
And should the bird fly back to thee
The cage didn't deny its liberty

Thalamus' Ink.

In this shadow shrouded rendezvous
A golden glow embraces you
But our conscience may set off bells
Impossible now to be ourselves...

Thalamus' Ink.

The Players Code

What else is there after I've got mine
Perhaps to get some more
There you are my mattress queen with
Fresh dew gracing your meadows and mounds
And a fractured smile now frames your sunlit face
Knowing my mind's flaw
As I arise

Endings echo for conclusions
Then search for new beginnings
And may these seeds
In yesterday's field
Lie fallow for another season
Shadows hide in the morning
To authenticate the truth
And may this door's closure
Confirm it

Thalamus' Ink.

Scream

Stunned into a future's uncertainty
Stunned and stung by such a tragedy
Stunned by a history of lost relations
Pervasive now these situations

Stunned by the emptiness
Neither mother nor wife
And asked to give up her baby's life
Not only that – but a part of her own
Rewarded now by being alone
Did you ever consider the depth of the pain
Which penetrates her again and again

She should have screamed
To the top of her lungs
But bit her lips
With you on her mind
To endure this scarring
For the rest of her years
Heroic she was without any cheers
And you walked away so blind

Did you ever cry
Or think of more than yourself
Or even say good bye
Blood, flesh and bones
In a plastic sac
No way now to bring
Her baby back

And will her mind
Or womb ever heal
Or when faced with intimacy
Will she squeal?
Or will I?

Thalamus' Ink.

When Love Hurts

Each time you say goodbye
Every time I've found that you've lied
Each time I'm stripped of my pride
And I've
Found myself
Still
In love with you

Thalamus' Ink.

Blue's Bruised and Half Buried Heart

The Blues
Is just depression's U turn
It's the voice that can finally mirror
The Soul's anguish
Outwardly

Thalamus' Ink.

The Pigment Solution

Itchy, prickly burning skin
Irritated outside and from within
Either aspect of the prism
Encases us within this prison

Even fair with flaxen hair
And no one the wiser until we speak
Then content is overridden by timbre
Doubtful now that it will engender

Yellow, red, black or brown
Arrives before a smile or frown
Never listened to and never heard
As if pigment itself speaks the final word

There's no graffiti upon this skin
The spoken word comes from within
If we are truly to stop and start
Words must reveal what's in our hearts

A difficult task casting off the past
And leaving the scab to heal
From inside out or outside in
Is there any way for us to win?

Perhaps if all pigment faded
Then as albinos all would live
With itchy, prickly burning skin
Irritated from outside but not from within

29

Thalamus' Ink.

Acid Rain

Witness this freak occurrence
No shelter from this acid rain
A high wire act on a razor's edge
While elephants trample upon my brain

Thirsting for the staple needed
The dollar now has superceded
Love from which we did feed it
Was our bread and water

Labor's mechanical monotony
Like raindrops pinging in my ears
Echoing long after the door closes
Hermetically sealing in my fears

Love's shower has less zeal
Lost its appeal
Less of me, no longer there
Leaving this ghost to consider the woe
Of the endless redlines that we toe

Life's futility mocks me
A repetition of yesterday
Slipping in mid-uphill grade
Leaving body horizontal
Head extended
Eyes straight up
And my assurance frayed
A pallbearer in life's procession
Eventual subject in death's parade

Love's residue is bequeathed in my 9 to 5
Bent on holding the line
Reward: needing 100 yet receiving 99
Pachyderms do pounce and cerebral spasms
Linger on
Muscles remain in tetanic contractions
This acid rain is never gone

Thalamus' Ink.

The Scavengers' Feast

Vengeance and Greed
Are the cancers set free
Hastening my departure
As they malinger and fester and breed
Oh malignant seeds

Buzzards in full flight
Descending concentric circles make
Reaper's scythe set in motion
A designated life to take

Day half done in a life all but dead
Satiety comes
When my carcass is numb
And the hyenas at last
Have been fed

Thalamus' Ink.

And The Band Played On

Mystic forces derailed Hades Express
Where eventually I will rest
Though scarred and bloodied I should be
Buried in this history
Which viewed us as a people most proud
Never again would our heads be bowed
Jubilantly expounding upon "Black Power"
In confirmation of our finest hour

The fear and thrill of renaissance
Minus all the ambiance
Music blaring and nostrils flaring
Dorms reeking of weed
Philosophizing about the struggle
And how we could succeed
Kent State's bullets in a hail
Students and demonstrators headed for jail

Attitude and aptitude kept the "pigs" in check
Fist raised as high as my Afro
Love beads about my neck
Clad in a dashiki and platforms
With others wanting to be
The Nigger – The Figure
The Mike Man – just like me
Power of the word
To be spoken
To be heard
To be jeered
To be hailed
For some to fight
For others to be jailed
Parents' pains – trailed their vacant looks
Drafted students don't need books

The reason for the riot
Some say yes, others deny it
Was in defiance
To proclaim
Our own self reliance

Thalamus' Ink.

I chose sanity
Over an insane number that could carry
Me to sea
And what in the hell were we fighting
And who was the enemy?

Martin, Jack, Malcolm and Bobby
Assassins camped out in the lobby
Leaders lost
Masses tossed
In an ocean of insanity
Questions on a nations mind
Of them and thousands left behind
Many of which we couldn't find
Whose war had they died for

And all the colors that went to fight
Returned to find injustice right
Where it had always been before
They went off to fight this war
Right at home and not next door

Many leaders sought political power
New factions formed by the hour
Many fizzled
Others lost force
I started riding that big white horse
Prestige's spotlight began to fade
As it's mount increasingly weighed
Thundering through this blistered brain
The steed I felt I could restrain
Bucked me off again and again
This happened so repeatedly
I'd take my friends along to see
Many who'd ride along with me

Thalamus' Ink.

From sugar to shit
From discrete to all over the streets
From an educated nigger
To how could you figure
From smoking grass
To out on my ass

Drool dangling down my cheeks
Catatonic for several weeks
Crawling again then finding stride
Recuperating some pride inside
From a basement with crack
To struggling to get back
The concepts that were once me
The sharing, the caring and the dignity

Why me?
Why was I set free?
Others had fought this war
Some I had heard of
Many I had ignored
Some returned and others stayed
For some we dug an early grave
None would be honored at any parade

Why me?
Why was I set free?
My education didn't protect me
Did someone actually hear my plea
Or just select randomly?

From teacher to preacher
From sinner to winner
Me- the brother who had done it all
Me-the casualty who survived the fall
Me-the cosmic conduit
Surely they'd listen to avoid that pit
As I stood upon the stage
An ugly crowd became enraged
They didn't come to listen to me
They came to hear the beat you see...
And the band played on...

39

Thalamus' Ink.

Anthem

We are still histories fools
Forever holding fast to yesterdays coat tail
While progress' fleet feet
Race ahead of the dust
Upon which we choke

Listen to our history
Touch the engraved misery
These are not our golden years
But lessons that spawned new lives
Our hells and purgatories
Our second and third comings
In the name of religion
And for a paper with burnt edges
That scorched and cremated and maimed

Awakened from past history
Pre shanghai – Pre landing – Pre lobotomy
Our lives demand their rightful restorations
It's time to reclaim our minds
It's time to leave the rat holes
It's time to vacate the crack in the walls
That left us crouched in corners
With edematous brains threatening
To implode

It's time to catch fleet footed progress
And stay one stride ahead
It's time for the seedling
Cast into the mire
To take root and blossom
It's time for horizontal sight
And the destruction of vertical gaze
In practice and in principle

Thalamus' Ink.

Life
Starts with thoughts of renaissance
Dancing in our heads
And it continues with positive toes
On the other side of our beds

RISE!

Thalamus' Ink.

Eyes On The Prize

World be still and let me natures silence hear
Though my sight slips behind veiled shadows
Others stand watch
Slumber is not this exhaustion's reward
For days fuse into a tedious procession
Illustrating my life's direction
A flesh assimilated cybernetic
Whose robotic movements
Trace the circle's destiny

Contour and conformity
Are now achievements' evaluators
Ills and inabilities
Fetch clones from incubators
Genetic engineers
Now demigods at the throttle
Detect defective D.N.A.
Then eliminate that model

Selective phasing out is already beginning
Once again who's to attend another wholesale thinning
Slumber is not this exhaustion's reward
Not til the "panacea" is totally explored
Cloning, like the atomic bomb,
Should sound an ear shattering alarm

World be still and let me nature's hushed silence hear
For life as it exist, may soon disappear
Yesterday's psychotic ideation
Now has plausible themes
And whose eyes are on the prize
Selecting the nightmares or the dreams
Though my sight slips beneath veiled shadows
Slumber is not this exhaustion's reward
Other eyes may stand watch
But are they better than the Lord's?

Thalamus' Ink.

P.C.

Left alone to his own devises
"Perfect Child" in his "Perfect World"
Computer loaded with Dungeons and Dragons
Not outside among kids with wagons

Self satisfaction in victory
Dictated by the body count you see
It's the total amount
In "Wolf" and "Die Hard Trilogy"

Rules are governed by computers
Nurturing the child's insensitivity
And there's no sense of morality
Just the final tally

The mouse is just a trigger
Zap – he's dead one less figure
Zap – then boom watch them explode
One more target then reload

Here winning isn't rising above
It's just elimination
If obstructed then it deducted
At his discrimination

Problems outside of his room
Handled in the same way
Press the mouse and zap the louse
Obstruction blown away

The only thing to vex ya
Is that the blood has real texture
And he can't reboot
And he can't reboot
And he can't reboot
Why didn't we interrupt him?

Thalamus' Ink.

FALLEN ANGEL

Thrust ashore by a raging storm
Too weak to walk
Too wet to keep warm
Too weak to eat without an assist
Her egocentric mother would resist

Perfect little angel from first cry
With perfect little wings
Yet unable to fly
As perfect as little angel could be
She couldn't control her own destiny

Life's already too brief
Angel was allowed one breath
Then wrapped in plastic and suffocated
Yes, she was put to death

Her mother's only fear in fact
Was being caught in the act
If angels aren't recyclable
Do demons stay to rule?

Thalamus' Ink.

SUPERMAN

We can't save
The slave called superman
Whose might is held tight in his hands
Whose greatest weakness is his brain
Which sprung a leak and won't work again

Leaping buildings in a single bound
Less success with us around
Failed "supers" have been found
Twisted bodies
Impaled on fences
Scratch one census
Mortal on ground
And the Krypton
Where's the krypton?

Brothers on the block
Selling a piece of the rock
But to whose foundation
And for what nation
The nation of the ducat
Oh f*ck it
The nation of the one
The nation of me
Devoted solely
For his own liberty

This "little situation"
Brought on his habituation
Now it's all he can do
To crawl back to his street guru
Flossing all the time
With just one thing on his mind
Super needs to fly
But someone brought the krypton by

Thalamus' Ink.

All alone on the throne
In his basement home
Expression on his face and his pace
Is a captioned tragedy for the human race
Thought he had it made
Until success was frayed
Then his depravity created a large cavity
A huge abyss – from listlessness to unconsciousness
Super has been played
Because that damned krypton stayed

Now – Every day's a dual
Every days' a dual
And where's the krypton?
It's what you're free basing – Fool!
Higher and higher
Higher and higher
Higher then expire
Splat!!

Thalamus' Ink.

Darwinism

Screams ring out from concrete buildings
Stretching towards clouds
Echoing and ricocheting without penetrating

Screams like colored ribbons wrapped about trees
Are peculiar only to perceivers
As masses of mutes
Forge and fumble forever forward
Bludgeoned forgetful and blindfolded

Securely wrapped in anesthesia's bliss
Stupidity's fortress beckons
And we follow the heedless and the headless
Like drunkards in serpentine fashion
To the gallows
To the chambers
To the electric chairs

Spawned from a world of concrete and steel
Broken sires and pregnant wombs without will
Dictionaries without definitions
Planes without destinations
Destinations without intentions
Intentions without focus
Focus without penetration
Penetration without love

Yes I raped the b*tch
And killed the mutha fu*ka
And now you sit there and stare at me
Yet you are the aberration

For I am spawned from this concrete and steel
From broken sires and pregnant wombs without will
This is my natural progression
Hell, I've never seen remorse

Thalamus' Ink.

And you judge me from atop your bible
With words without definitions
Whose intentions and focus are not meant
To penetrate these screams that ring out
From concrete buildings
Stretching toward clouds
Echoing and ricocheting without penetrating...
Listen to the rain pelting the marble floor

Thalamus' Ink.

Alone In Desolate Surroundings

He was selected for a mission into the darkest depths
Without the benefit of stars, planets or navigational instruments
For there were none

Survival remained his sole purpose and he held on
Even though there was little hope of reversal
As he drifted from life as he had known it

His cabin light was as weak as an old man's eyes
Main battery having long since failed
And auxiliary, now just right of zero

Coldness existed in varying degrees and its bite was irreparable
The cerebral games however, were even more devastating
He had recalled how his friends, now familiar strangers, and been afraid
inhale
around him and later folded their arms in his presence as if human touch were
the
vector. The half smiles had conveyed discomfort, aloofness and a healthy relief
in his
induction rather than their own

He had been out there so long that he wasn't even recognizable
So much older and frailer then his chronology
A ghost whose lone fraying thread to life was its need to breathe
For the soul was already in transition from a body
Barely large enough to house a humming bird
The epidermis now parchment thin
Virtually viewing viscera through onion skin

Hideous tattoos served as effective advertisement
And seemed to chart the course
This lifestyle consequence whether fated or selectively preferred
Brought on a hopelessness and devastation no one ever deserved
"Earth to voyager…
There's still nothing to report!"

11/1/97

Thalamus' Ink.

Through Life's Cracked Door

from infancy to infantile in protracted agony
perhaps an old man's epitaph or just his legacy
first breath and then his last revealed his only frailty

always strong in body and mind
undaunted by life's elements
that is until the present events
exhausted his cat – like nine
there's no turning back this time

his breath a broken metronome
dysrhythmic now until it's gone
heeding gabriel's blast and then at last
he'll be passing on

oh Powers that exist
quiet his heart and let him rest
take his soul and set him free
with me goes a part of him
and with him a part of me
with him a part of me

61

Thalamus' Ink.

Future Focus – Slow Fade

Complacency is failure's accomplice
Not progress's companion

Thalamus' Ink.

If *tomorrow's day were without light*
 Do you think that you've done all that you might
 To face past wrongs
 Weak or strong
 And endeavored to set them right

 Or *seeking the safety of an impregnable*
cocoon

 Are you destined to remain mum in the
womb

 Left all alone
 To pamper your own
 selfish soul

Thalamus' Ink.

"I"

I will rise to see
each morning's sunlight

With a heart of good intentions
and
With intellects clear head

And from the loins of thousands
a seed will spawn
To alter the "Mighty Mississip"

Whose course adjustment will find us
Black
and
Whole
and
Never again dotting
            The "I"

Thalamus' Ink.

Purpose or Reason

Beware the demon of the dollar
Whose sparcity could make you holler

And bond you tightly to your work
With insane hours driving you berserk

Setting all on a solo track
A mental state that does contract

Tunnel vision's your state of mind
And once wealthy you will find

That all of the riches you now see
Can't bring you back your family

This valiant shouldering of the plow
Whose rows became skewed some how

Thalamus' Ink.

Repose

Lie still my love
And for each days slavery
Welcome amnesia as its own reward
Lie quietly to stifle the sounds
That drove your pulse
And bruised your brain
That absorbed the affront
And strained this smile
That oft frightens clouds away
And deters all harbingers of darkness

Lie close to me
Life's most weary child
Trust this embrace
Like the eternal rhythmic tides
That cradled and carried you gently ashore
Enjoy this brief winter's slumber to convalesce
With the ensuing spring to rejuvenate
Recurrent dreams of hope and happiness
Frame tomorrow's daybreak
Arousing both heart and head
To face another day

6/24/99

Thalamus' Ink.

Conundrum

Mindless from which acorn
The strong tall oak will grow
Hard to detect
Which sprout in effect
Will cast the greatest shadow

Brawny branches and broad leaves
Offer comfort in harsh times
But never egotistically
Never by its own design

Never knowing how far
The shade of influence will spread
Never reneging on its role
Until at last it's put to bed

And those left unexposed
Seldom nurture acorns
From which the strong oak grows

Thalamus' Ink.

Soaring

Mystic eagle in your splendor soar
On strong undrafts or puff of air
Extended wings in smooth flight
Belie in reality that you care

From such a lofty celestial perch
Surely heaven you have found
But staring closely into your eyes
I've found them focused upon the ground

With accommodation exceeding men's
The slightest detail is magnified
Insight's integrity is never in question
Or your ideals would be defied

From gifts that the Lord has granted
This majestic eagle now has found
Weightlessness in his aerial environs
And equal buoyancy upon this ground

Prudently instructing inspired fledglings
In the art and care of how to fly
While avoiding the pitfalls of others
Who hit walls and then did die

Live and thrive endangered species
With many others taking to wing
Filling the heavens with soaring eagles
And lifting every voice to sing

Dedicated to Professor Cornel West
3/16/99

Thalamus' Ink.

Summer's Vintage

I remember the juvenile summers
Sun drenched kinder days
That lasted almost forever
Or until the dusk's gray haze
All of that time was truly mine
I'd lie and watch fields sway
And wonder where dandelions went
As their seeds were blown away
And did they live and thrive?
It was so good to be alive

I remember the torrid teenage summers
Playing on the beach
With seagulls screeching
As if they were preaching
And new what was on my mind
As I rubbed the lotion
In rhythmic motion
From your shoulders to your behind
Hormones in a nuclear reactor
Fission or fusion – whatever factor
Transistor playing all that jive
It was so good to be alive

I remember the family summers
And our children in the park
With baseball, barbecues
And amusement rides long after dark
Seeing their cheerful expressions
As we were flying a kite
Then frowns abound as the string unwound
Launching it out of sight
I recall how anxious they were
For the fourth of July to arrive
The love we had was more than some fad
It was so good to be alive

Thalamus' Ink.

Summer's set in 4 / 4 time
And marches so quickly now
The children are out of the house
And have found their niche somehow
Summer's past perfection
In retrospect brings sorrow
But exuberance will be rediscovered
The grandchildren arrive tomorrow

Summer's rpm's rev faster as you age
And the progression recedes to the background
From the center stage
But as long as there's a role
And I can amply provide
It stands to reason in any season
It's so good to be alive

When First...

My soul smiled when first I looked into your eyes
And my heart's happiness
Bounded into a place
That leaves minds weightless

I was enslaved by the timbre and rhythm
When first I heard your voice
Often it dictated and reflected
The richness and pace of our lives

A sacred purpose and direction evolved
When first I walked with you
And found our strides conformity
Just as our minds

I felt our strengths meld
When first I touched your hand
And felt that life's roughest seas
Would always be negotiable

Now in this morning's light
Realizing all we've manifest,
I close my eyes to pray a while
For surely I've been blessed

When now I look into your eyes
And you see your best in me
I know this time together
Is the best that life can be!

Thalamus' Ink.

A Mother's Love

Don't take me down those dusty roads
They've choked my lungs
And broken my heart
Memories of a distant time
Inflicted pains which won't depart

The thicket of a briar patch
Describes my wooly hair
While momma's was soft and light
And moved with a wisp of air

Momma's eyes were hazel
Mine are as black as coal
She was thought of as a princess
And I as an old soul

Momma's skin was silky cream
Mine is ashy brown
And I would wash it twice a day
But the color wouldn't fade away

Momma was always so calm
With me, fire rages within
As if fighting off demons
In a dream
Apparent heir to someone's sin

Lowest on the pecking order
Teased about hair, eyes and skin
Running home crying often
Momma would soothe the pains within

So off I went tilting windmills
Attempting to get away
On rainy days I stare out of windowsills
Remembering things she'd say

Thalamus' Ink.

"As long as there's life within you
My love and beauty will remain
But my daughter always remember
A woman's best feature is her brain"

How could mother and daughter
Contrast and contradiction be
For superficially, I loved her beauty
And she, profoundly the beauty within me

Thalamus' Ink.

Ode to a Liskin Urn

Today
More than a "Gift" did I receive
For once unwrapped
I felt it breathe
And I could never ever conceive
Of anything more beautiful

In awe I viewed this mystic urn
It matters not which way it's turned
Far or near – each and every view
Confirms the greatness of it's potter – you
Its shimmering glaze delights my eyes
With patterned stories of paradise
And some of pain and some of fear
That at times did appear
And yet you've left your history here

So was sent this talisman
Your sentry upon my parapet
Guarding all within its power
While reminding us how life does flower
To find you now within my house
Is to find us both at home
And so ... I smile

Thalamus' Ink.

Autumn's Glow

Have you ever witnessed the moon's intrusion
Upon the abbreviated sun
Serving notice to all with its noon debut
That summer's done and autumn's due

Have you seen last night's frosty epitaph
Imprinted on a window sill
Or felt the mornings shiver
As angels brushed by at will

Have you viewed nature's kaleidoscope
When trees of forest green
Assemble like a prism's rainbow
Accenting this festive scene

It's harvest time
And labor's deeds are manifest
It's jubilation and thanksgiving
Because we've all been blessed

With the dusk
We slow the rush
To view nature's play
In this scene our beauty queen
Is aroused from where she laid
Constellations and shooting stars
Serve as her entourage
And escort her on the way

This harvest moon needs more room
To flaunt her evening's glow
The yellow incandescence is effervescent
And fuses this celestial show

With light there is wisdom
With harvest there's reward
Stars are our ambition's goals
This beauty – it's the Lords

89

Thalamus' Ink.

When time arrives and its autumn
Or perhaps you're in "Act III"
May the aura you possess have autumn's glow
Or more intensity
And may you share your harvest here
Just as generously

Thalamus' Ink.

A Perfect Presence

Look beyond the words
Peer into my heart
Exposed and vulnerable
As flowers in full blossom
Or lovers in passion

Your love lifts me
Until the air becomes my ground
As solid as these feelings
We share with one another

Our breath and the winds
Were at once one
Both Servants and Superiors
Enchanted by the touch
Thrilled by touching

Your flavor
Rewards my tongue
With memory and addiction
Your fragrance is a bridal train
Of morning glories
That hover upon the winds
And saturates the dew
From which I drink and bathe

Stars are the celestial diamonds
Loves display dispersed across skies
That light
Upon and within us
Oh, that we had the power to bare
A catalyst to keep all here
Sustaining us on this solid air
While
Begging for
No tomorrows

Bliss abounds
Limitless
As in open fields
And we rise towards heavens
Without ceilings

Clouds are the mattresses
Upon which we lay
Freeing us of form
Leaving minds to stretch and wander
Far beyond ecstasy's path
To discover the supreme freedom and calm
Found in post orgasmic gasps

Thalamus' Ink.

Adieu

Woman
Are there no limits to a heart's sorrow
For you are already a long time gone
Icy winds chill in your wake
As old sol's smoldering embers
Smear our signatures across primrose skies
Muting the mauve horizon

Silence and numbness are momentarily twins
Though each would break the code
To speak or feel your breath again
Your tears once assured that blossoms reported
Then laughter teased and tickled leaves
Your hands once felt and fondled fertility's desires
Then love solicited and insured warmth and tenderness

Time destroys the evidence
Cloaking your fragrance in a bitter almond scent
Breaching my mind to rob you from me
With a potion dedicated to amnesia's scheme
Creating concentric ripples
Disfiguring all of my dreams

Now is the time of the haunting
And all is disemboweled
When the witch's wrath sears the harvest
Licensing barren fields
And trees to scream
Just like the reeds
As heckling winds fill their vacancies
Encasing all in crystalline glass
Addling once perceptive minds
Then putting all to bed alas

Thalamus' Ink.

From slumber
Was shook this fiendish scheme
Which fell to earth like a lifeless hand
Discovering your absence aroused some fear
That never again would you appear
If elopement's intrigue this time survives
Leave that potion by my side – adieu

∞

Thalamus' Ink.

Keep the light of knowledge bright
The sighted will see and follow
While the blind stumbling may feel its warmth
And then seek its source

Ruuummm
Ruuuuuuuuuuuuuuuuuuummmmmmmmmm
Ruuuuuuuuuuuuuuuuuuummmmmmmmmmmmmmmmmmmmmmmmmm
Ruuuuuuuuuuuuuuuuuuuuuuuuuuuuuuuuummmmmmmmmmmmmmmmmmmmmmmmmmmmmmm
mmmmmmmmm

Thalamus' Ink.

99

Printed in the United States
834800003B

9 780759 681330